DONGHIA
THE ARTISTRY OF LUXURY & STYLE

DONGHIA

THE ARTISTRY OF LUXURY & STYLE

Sherri Donghia

WITH KAREN LEHRMAN

BULFINCH PRESS
NEW YORK • BOSTON

contents

Design **fusion** *is the ultimate in creating a true reflection of who you are through your furnishings.*

About twenty years ago, my Parisian friend Marianne had a country retreat in Connemara, on the west coast of Ireland. One summer weekend, I went to visit her after finishing my work in the northern part of the country (I was consulting for fashion designer Paul Costelloe). I loved Ireland. I had never experienced a place of such peace and tranquility.

Marianne's home was an old rectory that she had only minimally modernized; quirky fixtures and furnishings now softened and complemented the dark-beamed ceiling and wide-plank flooring. On the walls of the entryway, an eclectic mélange of personal Polaroids were pinned in long, narrow rows, interspersed with miniature watercolors of the local vistas. The living room was anchored by a comfortable handmade English sofa, which was covered with several layers of Amish quilts and flanked by a pair of soft Irish tweed–covered club chairs.

I often think of Marianne's home as one of the better examples of what I have come to call design fusion — the merging and blending of different cultures, periods, and styles. For me, design fusion is the ultimate in creating a true reflection of who you are through your furnishings. It also never goes out of fashion and always feels believable and authentic. What made Marianne's home work so well, in fact, was that each piece — and the way they were all put together — exquisitely echoed the multifaceted personality that I loved and enjoyed about my friend: her home was rooted in her unique spirit and soul.

This authenticity gave her home a bold, effortless panache: it made her home look unstudied, totally relaxed and comfortable, which I consider key to great design fusion. There was nothing pretentious or "perfect" in the house. Local Irish antiques and ecclesiastical artifacts were combined with Bennington pottery from Vermont and mismatched English bone china patterns for the sole purpose, it seemed, of our physical and emotional pleasure. This melodic disharmony was never static, but always evolving, which I witnessed when the same elements were totally at home again, years later, in Marianne's Paris apartment.

At its best, design fusion will reflect an individual's

At its best, design fusion will reflect

an individual's signature style.

signature style. In fact, my other favorite early example of design fusion could not have looked more different than Marianne's. In the mid-nineties, I had the rare opportunity of collaborating with fashion designer Romeo Gigli on a textile collection for Donghia. Working with Romeo's

incredibly talented, multicultural design team, and seeing the fabrics executed by the skilled hands of Italian and Indian craftspeople, was a crash course in fusing the Byzantine and the Baroque, in melding the influences of disparate cultures to create a fresh design aesthetic.

But I probably learned just as much from spending time in Romeo's flagship retail store. When the fashion crowd traveled to Milan in those days, 10 Corso Como was the address of a must-see destination. As with his

FROM LEFT: Me, with my Parisian friend Marianne Rachline; **MIDDLE:** In Manila, with two of my design/production associates; **RIGHT:** Bloomingdale's ready-to-wear fashion office, in the early seventies: Judy Galloway, me, Katherine Murphy, Sue Wilson, Gay Vincent, and Anne Wightman.

fashion designs, Romeo's interiors proved to be relevant and refreshing: Arne Jacobsen "Egg" chairs upholstered in strong acid colors were juxtaposed with hand-embroidered Moroccan hassocks and candy-colored Venetian chandeliers; contemporary graphics and art by Kris Ruhs were peppered throughout; and the whole interior landscape was anchored by an assortment of multi-patterned kilim rugs. Romeo's clothing and accessories echoed the same exotic collage.

Just because great design fusion looks as though it were done with the sweep of the hand doesn't mean that it actually was. Underlying what makes both of these examples work is a basic understanding of the classic design elements — proportion, scale, and balance. This shouldn't be surprising: the greatest design throughout the ages is rooted in these universal principles — whether it's the timeless design of the klismos chair, developed by the ancient Greeks in the fifth century BC; the graceful Japanese

feel intimidating. Great design fusion, like nature, is far from perfect; the trick is to learn how to exploit imperfections to create authentic, layered beauty.

In this book I describe how we at Donghia interpret the four elements of good design — Form, Texture, Color, and Light. I also explain three concepts that give Donghia designs soul and authenticity: Design Integrity, Design Tension, and Design Balance.

When my cousin Angelo Donghia started his interior design firm in the late sixties, decorating trends went in the direction of either a stiff, sterile formalism or a hard-edged, soulless minimalism. Angelo, by contrast, took his influences not just from museums or historic homes, but also from fashion, the street, and perhaps most important, his own jet-setting lifestyle. The son of a tailor, he built his practice on the principle that interior furnishings should be constructed with the same precision and quality of a fine custom-made suit. But the shapes and patterns

Great fusion design, like nature, is learn how to exploit imperfections

kimono; or La Malcontenta, the perfect house for human scale, designed by Andrea Palladio in the 1550s.

Great design fusion is both sensual and sculptural, dramatic and artfully disciplined; the "fusion" is as much about balancing the rational and the emotional, the linear and the organic, as it is about the merging of different cultures. Rooms that are lacking a point of view tend to feel incomplete, while rooms that are too perfect often

that Angelo preferred were far more sensual, seductive, and bold than anything on the market: his goal was to make people look good and feel good in the private and public spaces that he designed.

So he began to design and distribute his own line of furniture and textiles, establishing Donghia's tradition of handcrafted, "custom-couture" furniture. Not surprisingly, the tailoring of the upholstery was of the utmost importance to Angelo — he molded the cloth to show off the lines, proportions, and details of the furniture; with the hand of a fine craftsman, he made sure the welts and seams were precise and crisp and the cushions fit the furniture frame the way a finely tailored suit skims the body.

Eventually, Angelo left a distinct mark on a wide range of interiors — from the Metropolitan Opera Club in New York City to the salons of the SS *Norway* to the homes of Ralph Lauren, Barbara Walters, and Diana Ross. Celebrities, cultural institutions, mass manufacturers, and leading corporations sought after his international style, characterized by simplicity of line, purity of materials, boldness of form, and sensual textures and shapes. Yet in all cases, Angelo's inimitable design sense proved as refreshingly original as it was appropriate to the person, place, product, or occasion. Angelo's creed was, "First of all, I design for people who require timely and timeless environments."

Bay in the Virgin Islands, the Grand Tetons in Wyoming, or The Boulders in Arizona, Mr. Rockefeller — who had his own museum-quality collections of arts and crafts from all over the world — seamlessly integrated each setting into its unique, individual environment. I learned as much about understated elegance as I learned about authentic design that is deeply rooted in indigenous cultures.

Today, Donghia produces original designs in furniture, textiles, trim, lighting, wallcoverings, and accessories, which are sold through architects and interior designers in more than fifty countries. By exploring the crafts and production techniques of different cultures around the world, we continue to merge classical proportions with multicultural influences, pushing the aesthetic envelope in the process. We have also broadened Donghia's unique emphasis on the handcrafted by adding hand-carved woods, hand-lacquered tables, and handblown Venetian glass to our custom-couture furniture line.

far from perfect; the trick is to to create authentic, layered beauty.

I was asked to join Donghia in 1987, two years after Angelo's death. I had been working as a design consultant for specialty retail shops and European fashion designers. My core client was Laurance Rockefeller, the founder and developer of the RockResort hotel group. Working with him was like taking a master class in design integrity — he truly raised the bar for creating the most natural, breathtaking vacation settings. Whether in Little Dix and Caneel

We like to think that Donghia's collections are both timely and timeless — bridging the gap between contemporary and traditional — yet far removed from ephemeral trends. The same can be said for great design fusion. If your design choices are truly rooted in both your unique taste and sense of pleasure, then your home will exude a serene elegance, a timelessness that will feel as authentic as each of your individual pieces.

CHAPTER ONE

Nature, travel, fashion, art — all provide *inspirations,* as does my ever-evolving reference library: the beloved objects and textiles I surround myself with.

DONGHIA

DONGHIA

MODERN COMFORT

I had just turned seven when design made its first appearance in my life. My parents were finished with

the building of our new home in Vandergrift, Pennsylvania, and were ready to start on the interiors. Vandergrift, I should point out, was not just any Smalltown, USA, but an iconic "paradise for the working man," designed in the late nineteenth century by Frederick Law Olmsted. Olmsted, of course, is far better known for the masterful creation of New York City's Central Park. But Vandergrift, with its gracefully curved, tree-lined streets, backyard gardens, and abundance of parks, has its own idyllic charm — and certainly inspired my lifelong enchantment with nature.

On one of those elegant tree-lined streets, my parents built a Federal-style house, with a portico front and dramatic bay windows. I remember being intrigued by all the talk of architectural detail and building materials, and began to feel a somewhat burning desire to offer up an opinion. The opportunity finally presented itself the day an interior designer from Pittsburgh arrived and emptied a

mountain of fabric swatches from his bag. I became mesmerized — obsessed really — by the seemingly infinite varieties of upholstery and drapery options.

Window treatments and bedding were my mother's favorite projects, so naturally they became mine too. I helped her select the layers of draperies for the front bay windows, beginning with Austrian shades in cream silk that magically filtered the light from dawn to dusk. Flanking the windows were floor-to-ceiling linen and silk drapery panels in pale silver and cream damask; these panels so captivated my cousin Angelo that he copied them for his first New York City apartment.

My mother instinctively understood the magic that can be created from pairing dissimilar textures in similar colors. She mixed rough cotton and linen weaves with crisp tailored silks — all in shades of cream, taupe, and winter white. Warm fruitwood furniture entwined with cool, creamy veined marble, on top of the coffee table and

around the fireplace. The result was both inviting and understated, elegant and comfortable.

Since I was a long way from being able to decorate my own home, my infatuation with color and fabric quickly turned into a fixation on clothes. All of Vandergrift soon became privy to my early creative exuberance, which was at times quite successful, other times perhaps less so. But it all paid off: after college I got a job at Bloomingdale's in New York City, as the assistant to fashion director Katherine Murphy — the doyenne of fashion retailing in the early seventies.

I went on to become fashion director of Gimbel's New York and then a product development manager for Federated Department Stores, designing everything from

Wabi-Sabi has enabled me to

intimate apparel to ready-to-wear and accessories. It was here that I fully began to understand — and champion — the idea of universal aesthetic principles.

As a small-town girl with big-city tastes, it was my role to argue, rather relentlessly, that it's not just people in urban centers who appreciate sophisticated design: people living anywhere in the world can appreciate great art and design — they just need to be exposed to it.

This job and the others that followed opened up for me the delights of world travel; perhaps most gratifying, I began to learn about diverse indigenous cultures and to find the incredibly talented local artisans within each. When I was the design consultant to Irish fashion designer Paul Costelloe, I made dozens of trips to Northern

Ireland. Most of his finely tailored clothing was constructed from hand-loomed woolens and linens from Scotland, England, and Ireland; the tailors, cutters, and sewers were the best of their trade, and they took great pride in the finished garments.

On each trip, I would spend a week working and eating meals with the local craftspeople, marveling at how simple and basic their lives seemed on the surface compared with my own hectic life. Their work had such complete authenticity that my eye became better trained in identifying honesty and soul in design.

Of course, I didn't have to leave the country to learn about authenticity. When I worked for the RockResort hotel group, it was my job to make each resort shop

appropriate for its location. Since the Arizona property had a wonderful assortment of authentic Native American jewelry and crafts, the annual market in Santa Fe became our shopping trip for the season ahead. The market was brimming with carpets, jewelry, baskets, and textiles as well as pieces from contemporary artists. Since we preferred the antiques for our RockResort clientele, we were always the first out every morning to buy the choice pieces. The people attending these markets were always dressed and accessorized in vintage Native American style; they became design and merchandising inspirations themselves.

Today, I travel about ten times a year (three or four times to Europe, at least once a year to a more exotic destination in Asia or Latin America, and the rest domestically). I try to capture as much as possible in notes, sketches, and photographs, which I use to make a scrapbook when I get home.

These scrapbooks are my muses. When my husband, Roger, and I were in Bali in the 1980s, he took a picture of women in their everyday local dress at a marketplace. Their randomly but artfully patterned batiks, stripes, and polka dots eventually turned into Donghia's Au Marché fabric. Visiting the Great Church of Hagia Sophia in Istanbul was my first dramatic exposure to Middle Eastern Islamic design forms, which have since inspired many Donghia designs, including Sophia, a geometric jacquard in silk, cotton, and viscose, woven to look like

Sabi asserts that imperfection is what gives an object its beauty and soul, and that art can best be understood intuitively, emotionally.

Wabi Sabi has enabled me to better trust my instincts and encouraged me to live even more sensually than I did before — appreciating the wonders of nature; the layered taste of every spice; the nuances of complex color combinations. It's also allowed me to better appreciate the different parts of my own personality — even if at times those parts feel contradictory.

Design fusion, I believe, is very much rooted in Wabi Sabi. Design fusion celebrates authenticity and sensuality, exploits imperfections, and encourages an intuitive creativity. Design fusion also happens to be as multidimen-

better trust my instincts.

molten metal mosaic threads.

To truly immerse myself in each new cultural experience, I try to go away from the protected environments and find the idiosyncratic villages. I look for the open-air markets — that's where the artisans are and that's where I find the quirky, one-of-a-kind handcrafted objects and textiles that I love to surround myself with.

My appreciation for the handcrafted was enhanced about seven years ago, when I discovered the Japanese philosophy of Wabi Sabi. Rooted in Zen Buddhism, Wabi Sabi celebrates the impermanence of the natural world. As a lifestyle philosophy, it teaches that true contentment begins with the acceptance of imperfections, both our own and everybody else's. As an aesthetic theory, Wabi

sional as we are — which is why it can have vastly divergent looks.

As you'll see, the two homes I share with my husband — a loft in Tribeca and a house on Long Island — could not look more different. The loft I would describe as urbane, spare yet opulent, and somewhat formal, while the Hamptons house is definitely more intimate, cozy, rustic, and bohemian. But, remarkably I suppose, each reflects parts of our personalities — and we feel perfectly comfortable living and entertaining in both.

I think this is one of the hardest things about design fusion to understand. Although it is a pastiche of different design vocabularies, the choice of pieces — as well as the way they are collaged together — has to reflect your unique style and tastes. This book can give you insights and inspiration, but the first step still needs to be taking a close, honest look at your personal style: what would it look like if it were to be transformed into a room?

It is also important to fully engage your senses. Don't just look, but touch, smell, listen. And travel! Go off the beaten path, see the "old" cities, visit the local craft markets and anthropological museums, and have a local guide or friend show you around. Of course, you can also travel through books and cinema.

I keep my senses engaged through the use of bulletin boards. I have elaborate boards in both my homes and at the office that are smothered with photos of interiors, paintings, architecture, fabric samples, bits of tree bark, even found objects. I never remove anything from the boards — everything just gets layered on top. At different times, these ideas will end up in some shape or form in my work or homes. I recommend that you hang up a bulletin board (or fabric screen), and pin up anything that appeals to you, visually or otherwise.

Living sensually is key to being able to appreciate design as both a rational and an emotional experience. You certainly need to understand the fundamental principles of proportion, scale, and balance, and in the next few chapters I offer up a few more design concepts for you to consider. But if your home is going to provide you with emotional as well as physical sustenance, if it's going to be your personal anchor, your safe haven — then you need to pay attention to how things *feel* as well as to how they look. Colors, textures, patterns, shapes — all can affect our moods in very unique ways; begin to take note of what makes you feel simultaneously calm and energized — serene. And there's one thing I believe none of us do well with: "perfection." We're not perfect, so why should we expect "perfect" homes to make us feel good?

Finally, don't try to rush into an "instant" décor. This is not natural, nor, in the end, all that effective. Designing a home is an ongoing, living project, and it should evolve over time. Just as you grow as a person and your lifestyle evolves, your environments should grow with you. Besides, the greatest joy and creative satisfaction lies in the process, not the end result.

Designing a home is an ongoing, living project, and it should evolve over time.

CHAPTER TWO

A work with design *integrity* exhibits coherence, character, and soul—authenticity. Every aspect is true to its unique identity.

Creating a home that looks within any design vocabulary.

even more so — you need to be able to merge vastly different styles, periods, and cultures.

For me, this challenge has induced a deeper, richer relationship with art and design, forcing me to think about what underlying factors unite all great works no matter what they look like and where they're from.

I've taken to calling the most basic of these factors design integrity. A work of design has integrity when every aspect — form, texture, color — is true to its unique identity and character: it is so well integrated you can see its soul. Frank Gehry's Guggenheim Museum in Bilbao has received a great deal of attention for its innovative, curvy facade and exotic titanium shell. But it also happens to be one of the most authentic works of architecture in recent times: every nuance speaks to a spirit of pure joy and playfulness.

Handcrafted objects — Venetian glass, embroidered and appliquéd textiles, hand-carved furniture frames — are almost inherently authentic: you can feel the artisan's spirit in every detail. Like nature (the prototype of authenticity), artisanal pieces are not flawless. But those tiny frays and crevices reflect the Japanese philosophy of Wabi Sabi: real beauty is rooted in imperfection. And the older a handmade piece is, the more beautiful and "alive" it becomes — the more it shows the patina of life.

Our world is so much about technology now that it's also comforting to live with something made by an artisan. The nondescript entrance to my loft is now covered with a hand-loomed striped wool fabric that lured me to it the minute I saw it at an exhibition in Milan. It was part of a collection of Bedouin textiles that were used in nomads' tents for warmth and decoration. The fact that

and feels unified is a challenge But with fusion design, it's

its life spans cultures and civilizations gives me as much pleasure as its intrinsic beauty.

But manufactured pieces can also have integrity. Look, for example, at the chaise on page 21. It is distinct and whole enough to stand completely on its own. Every detail — the perfectly pitched back, the finely sculpted silhouette, the slightly arched leg — speaks to its character. It has enough presence to be the center of attention and enough dignity not to require it — that's integrity!

What I don't believe falls into the realm of design integrity is the faux-authentic — either a piece that has been purposefully tattered, chipped, and distressed or a poor-quality imitation of a classic design. The magical patina of an authentic object is the result of years of loving wear and tear, which can't be artificially imposed.

You can find pieces with integrity at any budget and

in every design vocabulary. Indeed, authenticity can be found in objects from all over the world. This is not a coincidence. Since authenticity is such an integral part of nature, it's also an integral part of our universal aesthetic, appreciated by vastly different cultures on a keenly intuitive level. And because these pieces are so understated and unassuming, they are also chameleonlike — they can easily be blended with other authentic pieces.

I also use the words *integrity* and *authenticity* to refer to a home's overall aesthetic: you can't copy someone else's decorating style and expect it to look and feel believable in your home. Integrity in design is like integrity in people: it emanates from deep within. And it's only this level of authenticity that will allow you to create the "sweep of the hand" style that's such an integral facet of design fusion.

PAGE 21: Our richly textured Obi collection, inspired by authentic Japanese obis, features deliberately irregular weaves, knots, and twisted threads; these textiles are most interesting when layered together. **ABOVE:** An African bowl displays a few pieces of my bone and horn jewelry. Whenever I travel I look for handmade, one-of-a-kind treasures, often embellished with carnelian, turquoise, and silver, which then become a constant source of inspiration; on display, they also add another layer of interest to my two homes. **RIGHT:** Story Stones, one of our signature fabrics, is an intricately woven jacquard inspired by Zen meditation stones, which are often found in Japanese rock gardens. Here it's paired with one of our handcrafted Venetian glass vessels, called Japonesque.

Integrity in design is like integrity in people: it emanates from deep within. And it's only this level of authenticity that will allow you to create the "sweep of the hand" style that's such an integral facet of design fusion.

PRECEDING PAGE: In the entryway of a timber-peg house on the east end of Long Island, antique Japanese vessels and a vintage kimono subtly dramatize the clean lines of our Open Villa sofa, upholstered in mocha-and-cream woven jacquard, with wool sateen pillows.

RIGHT: In the living area of this house, two Donghia Gramercy sofas frame a coffee table made from an antique door. The serenely sculpted silhouette of the sofas provides the perfect backdrop for the subtle detail of the accessories — a Noguchi floor lamp, rattan fans, and oversized pillows made from antique Japanese indigo fabric mixed with Donghia's Sashiko. In general, I prefer this type of balance: clean (though not minimalistic) lines for the bigger pieces juxtaposed with uniquely exuberant accessories.

PRECEDING PAGES: Close-up of the table runner, which was made from Donghia's Shinano fabric and embellished with vintage keys. Our Anziano chairs frame the dining-room table, which consists of a slab of granite resting on roughly hewn wooden blocks. Japanese bronze candlesticks and a contemporary Japanese print continue the aesthetic.
ABOVE, FROM LEFT: Our cotton Indigo collection, inspired by vintage indigo cloth; with its geometric cutouts and perfect symmetry, the facade of our commode mimics the classic lines of the beautiful Italian villas designed by Andrea Palladio; antique cloths from Thailand, Africa, Japan, and South America fill the commode's drawers, and handmade Japanese artifacts enhance its surface; in the guest bedroom, an antique Japanese kimono adorns the wall while pillows in old Japanese textiles rest on a handmade quilt collaged with strips of our indigo fabric.

RIGHT: In the study, wicker and rattan Koga chairs set off a triangular granite-and-metal table — an early design by Comme des Garçons' Rei Kawakubo. Donghia's Saratoga sectional sofa, upholstered in Yumihama, and a sandblasted glass vase maintain the East-meets-West theme.

PAGE 37: In the foyer of my Tribeca loft, I've paired a Chinese red lacquer desk with our DiLorenzo side chairs in a vintage Donghia textile. Gracing the desk's top are an opalescent glass vessel and our handblown Medusa lamp, with a shade covered in Piega fabric. Underfoot, a hand-knotted Donghia for Odegard runner in Himalayan wool, and on the walls, our Hammered Silver tea paper. Metal leaf casts a warm and seductive glow onto both the room and the people in it. Made by artisans who lay out the thinner-than-tissue leaves of precious metal one sheet at a time, the paper has natural variations in texture and shading that become part of its beauty.

CHAPTER THREE

A "harmony of contrasts," design *tension* gives a room verve; at its best, it provokes the element of surprise.

You have no doubt seen how environment "alive," enchanting,

no doubt seen rooms that mix styles and cultures but the effect is ultimately bland: there's no energy or magic.

The difference between the two is what I call design tension — creating a "harmony of contrasts" with an intriguing and unconventional juxtaposition of shapes, textures, patterns, and colors. This kind of discordant harmony can be created through an endless number of innovative combinations:

• Sensual upholstery pieces mixed with the more severe lines of Shaker or Mission-style furniture;

• An intricately carved Chinese table supporting a simple handblown Venetian glass lamp;

• A delicate Louis XVI fauteuil upholstered in a rough natural linen;

• A vintage Knoll office chair upholstered in a sophisticated yet whimsical fabric (instead of the expected leather).

Not just any combination of contrasts will work, of course. Each of the individual pieces has to be authentic, able to stand on its own. And to create the "harmony" part, the contrasting elements need to be tied together in some way — through color, proportion, thematic pattern, or recurring motif. In my country house living room, I combine draperies with a folk-art peacock motif, pillows covered in hand-blocked Indian textiles, amber-colored Venetian glass lamps, and two contemporary prints by Christo. Using the above description, it would seem as though there is no apparent link between any of these things. Yet running through the various materials are different shades of tangerine, honey, and ochre, creating a subtle yet visually intriguing bond.

Objects can have design tension within them. Think about a sofa or table with straight lines except for slightly

design fusion can make an seductive. You have also

curved legs. Or an elegant, hand-loomed silk damask in an unexpected contemporary pattern and color.

Optimally, what you want to achieve with design tension is the element of surprise — a combination that's both unusual and striking. Try combining vintage and new fabric in the same pillow or throw. Or pinning an antique Indian door-hanging (a *thoran*) over an upholstered linen headboard.

Another way you can create design tension is through the element of whimsy — jacquard-woven fabrics with sophisticated yet whimsical motifs; a collection of candid black-and-white party snapshots; a set of dining chairs in the same pattern but in different colors (preferably two in each color for easy pairing). For the whimsical element to work, though, it has to be sophisticated and well executed.

Any design tension that is too extreme will take you out of the realm of surprise and into the land of shock, which is really not a place you want to be if you're looking to create a serene and timeless home. Adding pieces for shock value alone also feels contrived — the opposite of the unstudied effect that looks and feels the best.

Great design tension creates a true individual statement. By artfully combining elements that have deep personal meaning, you will add that unique layer that makes a house a real home. To me, there is nothing more off-putting than a perfectly styled interior, where everything matches tastefully. I much prefer a home that is truly lived in and that reflects the quirky personalities of its inhabitants. Human beings are not perfect or generic; neither should their homes be.

PRECEDING PAGES, LEFT: Further down my hallway, a Venetian glass lamp and various vessels adorn the veined marble top of my antique Italian console. A print by a contemporary Japanese artist and two Richard Giglio drawings complete the vignette.

RIGHT: Handblown glass creates instant dramatic tension with a variety of objects; it also humanizes spaces, bringing a bit of poetry into our lives.

THIS PAGE: My living room is anchored by our Gramercy sectional, upholstered in Astrakhan chenille; it also provides seating for at least eight! The sofa's clean lines set off an antique Christofle silver tray table, which supports an heirloom silver tea set and pre-Columbian pottery. And the vegetable-dyed terra cotta carpet, designed by Donghia for Odegard, adds literal and figurative warmth to the room.

PRECEDING PAGES, LEFT: Soft, sensual sunlight filters through my Swiss cotton scrim; the extra-deep hem is the exact height of my windowsill, creating a horizontal line across the entire wall. My favorite coin-silver Indian table, encrusted with semiprecious stones, is flanked by a pair of Eaton chairs in our Wildly Chic fabric.

RIGHT: Our Margarita dining chair, upholstered in a linen velvet, marks beautifully — creating instant patina. Some of my most treasured and unique accessories have been created by "collaging" my own personal antique textiles with contemporary fabric and trim; this gives new life to the beautiful scrap of old fabric that may otherwise fall into shreds. For this bolster, I paired vintage hand-embroidered textile fragments from Uzbekistan with Donghia's Wildly Chic. This sienna silk pillow features handmade metal fringe from our Decadence collection. Over the years I have collected a variety of examples of *zari* metal trim, but couldn't find handmade metal trim in the contemporary marketplace — until our special source in India convinced an entire village of craftsmen to revive this lost art.

AT RIGHT: My ten-foot-long table — a twenty-first-century version of the traditional harvest table — consists of three solid zebrawood planks. Red lacquer candlesticks from a trip to Kyoto offer some vertical balance, while handblown Venetian glass stemware and Indian sari placemats complete the setting. On the sectional lies an antique Venetian wall hanging with *zari* embroidery, which I backed with Donghia silk to give it stability.

ABOVE: An illuminated floating shelving unit, which Angelo Donghia designed in the seventies, displays my collections of mercury glass, red coral, Burmese and Nepalese lacquerware, as well as a hand-painted Tibetan chest. The Hammered Silver wallcovering adds an extra layer of luminosity. **RIGHT:** In the living room, a Chinese altar table, adorned with jeweled Turkish and Thai headpieces and a German anglepoise lamp, serves as my breakfront. Hanging above are antique textile fragments, which I had matted on natural linen.

ABOVE: Whimsical tension is created by combining an oversized watercolor by Richard Giglio (a friend, exceptional creative talent, and fine artist) with our signature Housepets fabric, here on one of our chairs. **RIGHT:** The freestanding wall in my dining area is stucco Veneziano — a combination of paint, marble dust, and wax that turns into a highly textured, dimensional sculpture on the wall surface, adding great patina and depth. I asked the artisan to create the color of crushed capers and black olives. In front, a Chinese demi-lune table with handsome latticework detail supports handblown Venetian glass vessels.

LEFT: An example of tension within the same piece: our handblown Venetian vessel infused with gold leaf holds a random accumulation of thistle flowers. I like to use unusual flowers and leaves, and to display them in a natural, uncomplicated fashion. **ABOVE:** In my Tribeca bedroom, the upholstered headboard contrasts with an African quilt, set into our Snake Chain fabric, and a bolster made from gold embroidered Indonesian cloth. Floor-to-ceiling linen drapery filters the southern light.

Optimally, what you want to achieve with design tension is the element of surprise — a combination that's both unusual and striking. Try combining vintage and new fabric in the same pillow or throw.

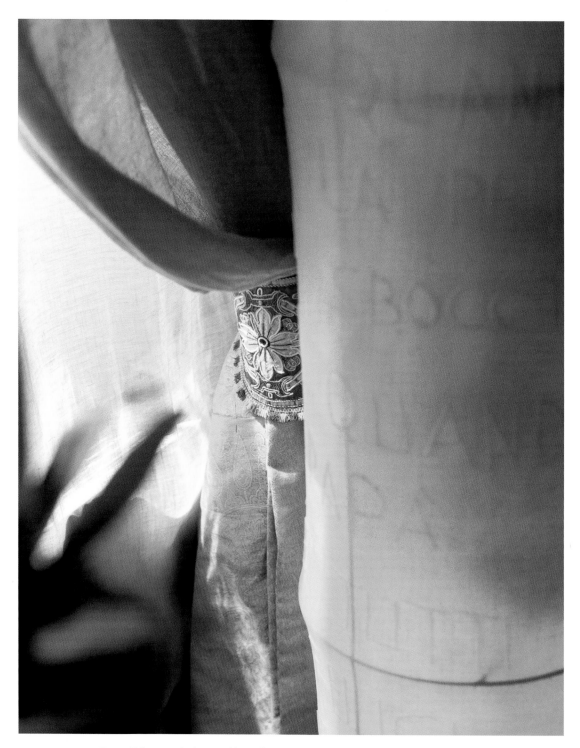

ABOVE AND RIGHT: In my Tribeca study, layers of linen drapery, held back by an antique Venetian textile fragment, filter the afternoon light. Contemporary Italian latex floor lamps, notched with poetry, serve as my other main lighting sources, along with an antique Venetian chandelier, reflected in our contemporary Venetian mirror. Against the wall sits the prototype for our Villa sofa, which serves as a perfect display for three pillows with eighteenth-century Ottoman embroidery. The gold painted-canvas chair is a vintage Donghia piece.

RIGHT: Also in my study, an ornate Indonesian display cabinet is surrounded by animal prints, matted in vintage Donghia textile, and "reverse-glass" paintings from Indonesia. An upholstered chair and kilims from Turkey complete the ensemble.
ABOVE: Inside the cabinet, I display personal family photos with an assortment of decorative glass tumblers.

CHAPTER FOUR

Through visual discipline, rhythm, and sensuality, design

balance

quietly blends tranquility with passion.

Since fusion design encompasses there's often a fine line between

serene ambience and unadulterated chaos.

To make sure you're heading for the former and not the latter, you need to achieve what I call design balance. This involves three things:

1. Visual discipline. "White space" is at the core of great fusion design, and yet it is one of the hardest things to allow for. If you're drawn to collecting exotic pieces and fabrics (as I certainly am), you probably feel the desire to display everything you own — for the enjoyment of both yourself and others. But we all need to be able to edit pieces out.

One way to both see your collections and not see clutter is by changing your accessories seasonally. This has the added benefit of continually adding new energy to the space, so that it never feels static. Another trick is to create groupings of similar objects — vases, shells, photographs. If you were to disperse these pieces throughout the room, they would create disarray as well as lose their impact.

2. Asymmetry. A room with too much symmetry — perfectly matched sets of chairs, tables, lamps, bookcases, mirrors, and the like — can be visually uninspiring. But asymmetry doesn't mean just randomly placing pieces about the room! Asymmetry also involves balance, though in a more complicated, abstract way. For instance, one oversized vessel on one side of the mantel could asymmetrically balance two or three small pieces on the other side. For asymmetry to work, though, you need at least one element — color, texture, or shape — connecting the two sets of objects.

Your environment should have a steady though

so many diverse elements, creating a stimulating, yet

unpredictable "rhythm." When your eye travels around a room, it naturally settles on various focal points — that's the rhythm. If a room is too "perfect," the rhythm will be flat. If a room is too cluttered or too chaotic, the rhythm will be unsettling. What you're aiming for is a nice cadence, with a hint of the unexpected.

3. Sensuality. Finally, you need to achieve a balance between the organic and the linear. Curves are seductive and feel familiar — nature is full of them, after all. But a room with nothing but curves is going to feel dizzying. The opposite — all straight lines and angles — feels too hard-edged, lacking both comfort and warmth. A good balance between the two will integrate a room, creating a tranquility that's deeply sensual.

Again, the end goal is the unconventional, the element of surprise. Pin a little quirky sketch in the center of an oversized gilt frame from the flea market; use pushpins to hang a series of postcards at eye level along a hallway; fill an entire cabinet with blue and white pottery of various shapes and sizes, from the minuscule to the grand. The truth is, you don't need to be an artist or a professionally trained decorator to achieve design balance. Just consider the everyday elements in your home your visual tools and move them around to experiment. My own homes don't look the same for more than a few weeks — I continually introduce new elements and remove others. For me, it's the ultimate creative outlet — fun, interesting, and deeply rewarding.

PREVIOUS PAGES: Symmetry can often balance out a variety of shapes and sizes. In the living area of this Fifth Avenue apartment, a distinctive William Kent console is flanked by a pair of club chairs and two dramatic Richard Giglio paintings.

THIS PAGE: The Chinese Coromandel lacquer screen gives this room vertical balance, setting off the Chippendale sofa, club chairs, and brass floor lamps, while the neutral upholstery blends quietly with the elaborate screen and rug. The layering of trays and tables of different periods and styles provides an unusual asymmetric tension.

RIGHT: Two trios of Venetian glass vessels, one clear, one opaque, offset each other in the midday sun. I have found that odd numbers work better for grouping objects of different sizes. Our handblown glass collection is produced on the small island of Murano, which has served as the center of Venice's treasured glassware industry since the thirteenth century. In creating these updated designs, we strove to continue in the timeless tradition, balancing a Renaissance opulence with an exquisitely modern sensibility. I have the utmost respect and admiration for the master craftsmen who create these one-of-a-kind pieces; their art challenges us to keep exploring new designs and ideas.

ABOVE AND RIGHT: A recurring motif can also provide balance — in this apartment, diamonds tie a variety of styles together. Here in the bedroom, diamonds become mirrors, adorning the built-in wall units. The duvet is made from a neutral-toned silk embroidery that we like to call "India couture." The freehand pattern offsets the geometry of the upholstered headboard.

CHAPTER FIVE

Form—

"good bones"—provides the foundation for innovative beauty; it's the designer's interpretation that gives a piece its soul.

In the fashion world, we call it "good lines" — if the construction and silhouette

of a dress or suit aren't right, it doesn't matter how great the color or pattern. The same of course is true for furniture. If the lines or "bones" of a sofa or table look clumsy or disproportionate, they will fatally detract from the most fabulous fabric or finish.

But while everyone in the design world may talk about the necessity of good bones, it's hard to get someone to actually define the concept. I believe that's because proportion in design is like rhythm in music: all humans are drawn to it intuitively, and when you see a false "note" you instinctively know.

The ancient Greek philosophers had a rather complex explanation for this phenomenon. They believed that a certain proportional ratio — what has come to be called the Golden Mean — can be found throughout the natural world, including in the human body itself. In a nutshell, the Golden Mean — also known as the Divine Proportion — results when the ratio of small elements to larger elements is the same as the ratio of larger elements to the whole.

As I understand it, because our ancestors evolved in the milieu of the natural world, we are instinctively drawn to objects that mimic natural shapes — and we find them aesthetically pleasing and comforting. As a result, artists and architects throughout the ages — from Leonardo da Vinci to Picasso and Le Corbusier — have either consciously or unconsciously used the Golden Mean in their designs. Take a look at the ancient Greek Parthenon and the design of a violin — you can see this distinct proportional ratio quite clearly in both.

When talking about furniture, though, it's important to remember that the best-designed objects are only *grounded* in classical proportions: it's the designer's interpretation that gives a piece character and personality — that pushes the aesthetic envelope. Traditional designs typically have great proportions, but the lavish details sometimes don't allow the soul to breathe. At the other extreme, minimalist design often removes the poetry along with the details.

I like to use the words sculptural and seductive to describe well-designed furniture. Optimally, pieces should look great from every angle — 360 degrees. With these compelling silhouettes, you can create presence and impact with fewer pieces: think about a fabulous upholstered chaise longue floating in the middle of the room, accompanied only by a floor lamp and a stack of books, all anchored by a sumptuous Himalayan carpet.

Not coincidentally, sofas or chairs that have good proportions tend to be the most comfortable. If you've ever sat in one of those exaggerated high-backed numbers that turn up in trendy restaurants and hotels, you know what I mean. In our Donghia design studio, we spend a great deal of time perfecting the "pitch" of a chair: the relation between the reclining angle of the back and the crown of the seat. Seat depth is equally important: the lower the seat, the deeper it should be. When a chair offers proper lumbar support, you can really feel the difference in your lower back.

Of course, a sofa or chair can have great proportions yet still not "fit" your unique anatomy. So don't be shy about trying it on for size — sit and lounge in different positions and actually put your feet up on the sofa, ottoman, or chaise. Being comfortable in your home is like being comfortable in your own skin — once you get there, the result will last a lifetime.

It helps of course if the materials and construction are also high quality: look for top-grade hardwood (mahogany, maple, oak, walnut). Do bear in mind, though, that wood is living and organic with a naturally irregular pattern, color, and texture. Wood finishes — lacquer, oil, wax — must look authentic and believable (and if possible be applied by the experienced hand of a professional).

Optimally, the frame of your sofa, chair, or table would be constructed of solid wood and fine veneers with as few joints as possible (the more joints a piece has, the weaker it's going to be). For example, a custom-couture Donghia chair has a frame that is double-doweled, glued, and corner-blocked, and the feet are part of the frame, not screwed onto it — a rare detail nowadays.

I truly believe that well-designed and well-constructed pieces are worth the investment for generations to come. If new pieces are not in your budget, though, you can always find older well-made and well-designed pieces at local auction houses, antique stores, vintage stores, or yard sales. Fine upholstered pieces are typically not expensive and can be reupholstered. And recycling makes ecological as well as financial sense: interior furnishings are the number-one contaminator of our landfills.

The shape, scale, and layout of your rooms provide the foundation for your furniture. Unfortunately, most of us don't have the luxury of reconstructing our existing houses or apartments, or starting from scratch — all we can do is learn to make the most out of the existing shape of each room. Here are some of my suggestions:

• Since light and space are the most precious elements of an environment, look at and live in a room before deciding what space you want to keep, not what space you want to fill.

• Highlight the room's best feature. If you have high ceilings, you can hang a dramatic chandelier and apply a silver or gold leaf to the ceiling. If you have a handsome, well-proportioned fireplace, you can flank it with a pair of wing or club chairs to create a strong symmetrical statement and a cozy "room-within-a-room." A great idea is to add a low bench to this vignette for stacking books, trays, and writing materials.

• Don't always assume a sofa should be pushed up against the wall. Try floating two mirror-image chaise longues or sofas in the middle of the room, anchored by an oversized carpet and lit by floor or table lamps.

• For true versatility, try a pedestal table with a round top and cloth to the floor: it can create an intimate dining area, a staging surface for drinks and desserts, or an impromptu desk.

PAGE 73: Donghia's Klismos chair reinterprets the classic Greek chair with sleek, sculptural lines that look good from all angles. Ergonomically correct with a plush upholstered seat, it is also a very comfortable piece.

ABOVE: In the den of a downtown Manhattan apartment, our sleek and modular furniture shows perfect form.

RIGHT: The asymmetrical Island sofa sports a trapezoidal base, meant to be accessible from both sides.

ABOVE: Our subtly curvaceous Shell chair and ottoman are embellished with silver and copper bullion fringe. A stack of goatskin books, serving as a mini-table, completes the vignette. **RIGHT:** The shallow tufting on our signature Grand Eaton chair, upholstered in wool Glacé, adds a refined sculptural element, as does the slight arch in the exposed wood. The table lamp complements the chair with its own sensual silhouette.

PRECEDING PAGES, LEFT: The dramatically seductive lines of this vessel mimic those of our Odeon tub chair.
PRECEDING PAGES, RIGHT: Our Mado table, maple with high-gloss lacquer on the inside, recalls the circular drum pits used by traditional Indonesian musicians. **ABOVE, FROM LEFT:** Our hand-chiseled Increspato lamp was inspired by the choppy waters of Venetian canals; the writing desk features a sleek Art Deco shape and legs that taper into brass or nickel sabots; a close-up of our DiLorenzo side chair, which has a stacked welt detail and octagonal front legs; our Phantom side chair upholstered in Piega shows off the signature Donghia leg — subtly and gracefully curved.

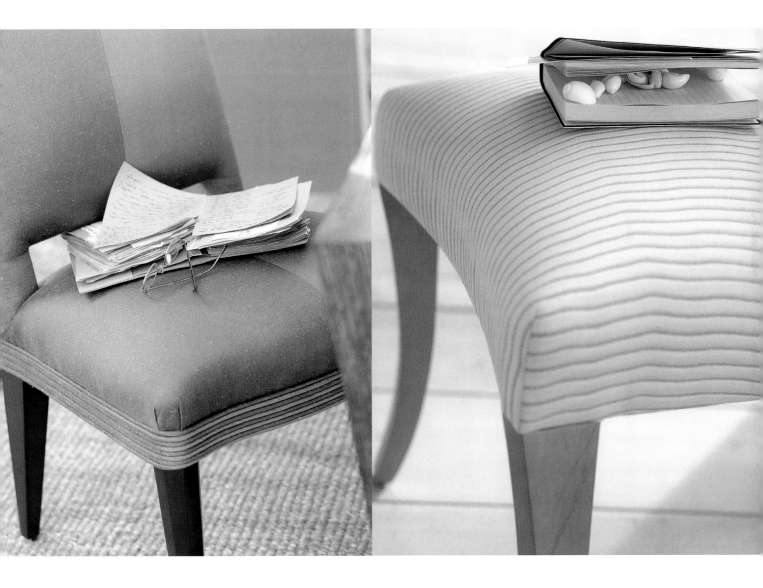

RIGHT: This club chair features a ribbonlike curve of wood floating over the upholstered arm, reminiscent of the wooden bridges built in rural nineteenth-century America. The wood is subtly angled to the outside to best fit the forearm. Instead of typical chair feet, a plinth-like wooden base runs along each side, following the chair's organic curves. The chair is upholstered in wool velvet.

ABOVE, FROM LEFT: A coffee table in birch emits the most delicate curves, reflecting nature's ethereal beauty; the Koga end table, inspired by the quiet sensibility of Japan's rural villages, is part of our indoor wicker and rattan collections; our Merbau club chair, which takes its name from the Indonesian hardwood used for the details, allows the natural tendencies of the wicker to help dictate the weave, and an end table, made of white oak, features a Brancusi-inspired pedestal column; a walnut table echoes the mid-century modern enchantment with form following function: its two-thirds enamel surface resists water, cold, and heat — a perfect place to put a snack and beverage.

Being comfortable in your home is like being comfortable in *your own skin* — once you get there, the result will last a *lifetime*.

PRECEDING PAGE: In the dining area of this downtown Manhattan loft by interior designer Laura Bohn, handsome upholstery mixes well with mid-century modern pieces.
THIS PAGE: In the living area, the high ceilings and floor-to-ceiling windows give the furniture room to breathe. The tightly upholstered lines of the club chairs (at left and at right) are pared down to the essence, while large loose feather and down pillows invite immediate relaxation.

CHAPTER SIX

Texture

is a designer's aphrodisiac. It seduces and ensnares, offering endless visual and tactile pleasures.

I grew up associating textures

My bedroom carpet was a velvety turquoise wool, my first official design edit. Braided white wicker furniture with cocoa and white calico cushions accented the plush rug, along with a unique Scandinavian school desk that featured the world map as the writing surface (thus my early yearning for nomadic travel!).

My summer bedding consisted of cotton sheets with a hand-crocheted border and white nubby-cotton "Martha Washington" spreads that felt light and cool, while my winter bed had heavy natural linen sheets that my mother had specially made. A channel-quilted silk duvet in chocolate brown completed the winter ensemble.

Texture is a designer's aphrodisiac. It seduces and ensnares, offering endless visual and tactile pleasures. Adding layers of opulent texture is the fastest way to create depth and character — to make any space more personal and intimate. But design fusion in particular requires a virtual cornucopia of dissonant tactile sensations: from gutsy linens to cobwebbed sheers; from precious silks to earthy cottons; from hand-rubbed woods to glossy lacquers; from fragile, etched glass to roughly hewn granite; from soft, buttery leathers to coarse horsehair; from cold, smooth stone to porous cement.

Fabric is the easiest and most effective way to change your environment. You want to create a good mix of the plush (velvets, chenille, mohair), the smooth (poplin, chintz, sateen), the nubby (tweed, bouclé, embroidery), and the organic (linen, hemp, raffia). A common mistake when first exploring fusion design is to overemphasize plush or pile fabrics. Not only can this feel too heavy and warm, but a full range of tactile sensuality engages all the senses: you want your fingers to be as stimulated as your eyes. Also, plush fabrics tend to absorb light while smooth-surfaced textures are more reflective.

Linen is my favorite — I love how it marks and wrinkles in all its variations: linen terry cloth, linen velvet, linen chenille, linen bouclé, linen gauze. My mother loved the comfort of linen as well and took great pride in ironing our sheets — a tradition I keep to this day. Nothing feels as clean and crisp as freshly ironed linen sheets. (And because linen is naturally antistatic, it actually repels dust!)

WEAVE STRUCTURE

Look for classic weave structures that are strong, balanced, and tightly woven — like a plain basket, twill, satin, herringbone, or crepe. These constructions will be more resistant to pilling and abrasion. But don't forget: any weave with natural fibers — linen, silk, wool — is going to have some "imperfections"; not only are these part of the natural yarn structure, but they should be appreciated for their imperfect beauty.

HAND

"Hand" means how a fabric moves and feels. Even smell is a factor for true aficionados. When I was consulting for Paul Costelloe, representatives from the textile mills would bring their latest creations to us for inspection. Paul would touch, crumple, and smell each wool and linen textile to find out how it would react to both the sewing and wearing. One day, our hand-knit sweater source from the Aran

Islands appeared with wool freshly sheared from his sheep. Since the natural lanolin from the animal was still in the fibers, the wool had the most amazing smell and feel!

DRAPE

Drape refers to how a fabric hangs or falls. For me, the flowing, chalky white curtains shielding Venice's Piazza San Marco from the late afternoon sun are probably the best example of unpretentious dramatic drape. Drape is most important for window treatments, table covers, and skirted beds. For a fabric to fall well, it has to have a certain weight. Ask to see as large a piece as possible to study how it falls from different angles (as well as how it reflects light).

UPHOLSTERY

• Consider upholstering an antique fauteuil with a whimsical jacquard pattern to create both design tension and an individual statement. Or put an old cotton Fortuny print on a new slipper chair.

• Dress a classic mid-century modern chair in a colorful wool sateen instead of traditional black or white leather.

• Use a different fabric in the same color family for the corner pleat of a bedskirt: for instance, with an eggplant silk taffeta, use an iridescent fuchsia inset.

WALLCOVERINGS

• Consider a more textural background for your walls, like paperbacked silk, linen, raffia, grass cloth, or hemp in countless shades of skin-flattering tones.

• Be totally extravagant with a ceiling of handmade gold or platinum leaf tea paper. My cousin Angelo often used this trick in dining spaces, bathrooms, and entryways because it casts a warm and seductive glow onto the room and the people in it.

• For bathrooms, kitchens, children's rooms, and dens, try low-maintenance vinyl wallcoverings in nature-inspired patterns and textures.

WINDOWS

• Layering is key for windows: Layer with different textures and weights but compatible colors.

• A drapery treatment can be simply lined or lined with an additional layer of cotton flannel to give it extra body for a really luxurious drape (especially good for floor-to-ceiling window treatments).

• Look for textiles that filter and diffuse the light — such as linen scrim, sheer cashmere, or silk or cotton mosquito netting.

• Never skimp on fabric; rather, overestimate how much you'll need.

• For added effect, "puddle" your draperies on the floor, and/or border them in a contrasting color.

PILLOWS, THROWS, TABLE COVERS, ETC.

• Combine different types of fabrics that work well together in monochromatic colors: rustic linen and silk damask; cotton velvet and linen chintz; felted wool and silk shantung; rustic African Kuba cloth and wool mohair.

• Change pillows, tablecloths, throws, and slipcovers with the seasons, or whenever you feel a room needs new life.

• Instead of buying ready-made duvets and throws, make your own textile collage in materials you like. Here again you can combine vintage and new fabrics.

PRECEDING PAGES: Diverse tactile sensations calm our minds and delight our senses. The understated, textured silk and subtly abstract patterns of Kimono work with all design vocabularies. Each of the twelve vibrant patterns in our Block Print collection is hand-printed in India on a textured cotton using carved wooden blocks — in the same manner Indian artisans have worked for centuries. **ABOVE:** Printed raffia wallcovering mimics the texture of the armoire and club chair. **RIGHT:** Inspired by the moods and rhythms of the plains of eastern Africa, Nairobi is part of our nature-inspired outdoor/indoor fabrics. Woven from Sunbrella® yarns, it is both resistant to stain and astonishingly soft to touch.

RIGHT: Angelo Donghia's former house in Key West was renovated to revive his signature casual, comfortable elegance — a look that works year-round in any climate. The stripped-pine living room now features signature Donghia elements: an Island sofa, Indonesian teak cocktail table and screen, Klismos chair, and Anziano stacking chairs. Layers of natural hemp and fine cotton sheers filter the tropical sunlight.

FOLLOWING PAGES: This exquisite silk base cloth is made from Tussah silk — a type of raw, natural silk with real character and patina. Atop the Zig Zag console sits our Venetian glass lamp, whose undulating bands of clear glass and silver leaf recall the sensual curves of a yacht slicing through water and the play of the wind in its sails.

ABOVE: Our bamboo-textured vinyl wallcovering provides a natural backdrop for a look of island elegance. The rich textures of basic plants and plant pieces — palm leaves, branches, sticks — add to the cool informality. **RIGHT:** The checkerboard ceramic tile in the master bath is a signature Angelo design element. **FOLLOWING PAGES:** A close-up of our Block Island weave, hand-woven over a hardwood frame. The bedroom features a wicker bed with a duvet cover in Espadrille, a handwoven Indian striped cotton that calls to mind the casual chic of the Côte d'Azur. The Lakehill chaise is celebrated for its unusual comfort — a lumbar support for the lower back is incorporated into the frame.

Fabric and trim are the easiest and most effective ways to quickly change your environment.

PRECEDING PAGES: These are the original South American hammocks, relaxing by themselves outside of my Hampton house, which inspired a collection of handwoven striped fabrics. Our Studio X chairs in several colorways of Espadrille surround my outdoor table, which is covered in a patchwork of textiles. I've layered my brick patio with Turkish kilims.

RIGHT: Along my sun-bleached wooden deck sit teak chaises with channel-quilted pads — each with a different color Sombrero stripe, inspired by the textiles of Guatemala and Central America. Woven from Sunbrella® yarns, these outdoor fabrics are resistant to not just stains but mildew, chlorine, and atmospheric chemicals.

FOLLOWING PAGES: We call our house Whispering Pines — it's serenely set within the largest white pine forest in New York State. This sylvan beauty dictated both the interiors and exteriors of the house: I wanted it to look and feel as natural and relaxing as the whispering pines themselves. A Nairobi-padded teak chaise works well with oversized bamboo candles.

PAGE 117: Chenille fabric reimagines the variegated rockscapes of the American desert as a luxurious corduroy.

Adding layers of opulent texture is the fastest way to create depth and character — to make any space more personal and intimate.

PRECEDING PAGES: The rustic, relaxed finish and gutsy weight of this linen cloth give it an air of unstudied chic. The station stripe throw, inspired by the techniques and patterns of ethnic jewelry, is hand finished with a fringe of Venetian glass beads. Here we combine a variety of weaves and clusters of chenille with metallic threading to create a fabric just as "alive," striking, and unique. **ABOVE AND RIGHT:** In my country bathroom, the chair and ottoman are upholstered in a cotton/linen blend with a modern abstract motif inspired by a nineteenth-century Chinese baby carrier. The folding screen is made from vintage flour sacks.

ABOVE: Our rather majestic daybed in silk, linen, and chenille. Inspired by the rich artisanship of Renaissance Tuscany, the fabric has the look and feel of antique gold-stamped velvet. **RIGHT:** The word *astrakhan* is used to describe the curly fur of a young lamb. Donghia's chenille version mimics the super-plush look and exquisite hand of this lambswool, though it is made from a sturdy combination of rayon and cotton. **FOLLOWING PAGES:** This jacquard evokes the rich, decorative forms of the Near East and is used here to upholster this minimally detailed slipper chair. The bronze trim, though opulent and surely decadent, has no trouble brushing up against this rough and humble hemp Odegard rug.

Of all the decorative elements,

color

is perhaps the most intimately linked to emotional experiences and moods.

Ochre — building facades in Tuscany. Celadon — the jades in Taipei's National Palace Museum.

Amber — the Amber Room at Tsarskoye Selo, just outside Saint Petersburg. Turquoise — Native American jewelry. Chalky winter whites — Swedish wood antiques. Coral red/oranges — the Sorrento Coral Museum of Terranova. Pink — Lecce, Italy, where the baroque buildings are made of pink stucco, marble, and stone, and also Jaipur, popularly known as India's "Pink City."

I travel to discover and absorb color: lush, exotic, sensuous colors then become imprinted on my brain, invariably bringing me back, emotionally and aesthetically, to their place of origin. Of all the decorative elements, color is perhaps the most intimately linked to emotional experiences and moods.

The ancient Egyptians as well as Native Americans used color and colored light for healing, and science is finally beginning to confirm their intuitions. Evolutionary psychologists believe that blues and greens tend to calm us because our brains associate them with tranquil seas and leafy forests. Studies suggest that viewing verdant landscapes can slow the pulse rate and lower blood pressure within five minutes. Oranges and reds tend to warm, energize, and excite us, as they are linked with fire and sunlight. White is what we see when all the colors come together in perfect balance, representing purity, simplicity, and serenity.

Not coincidentally, colors that most closely resemble those found in nature tend to create the strongest emotional impact. I call these colors "complex" because they are rich, subtle, and layered — an olive or sage rather than a Crayola green; cocoa or mahogany rather than a flat brown; turmeric or saffron rather than a taxi-cab yellow. In general, I like to surround myself with earth and sea tones with great character and patina — indigo, henna, turquoise, coral, ivory, and amber.

Once you start looking for color complexity, you'll see that you're more apt to find it in textures like heathered Shetland wools, multicolored tweeds, and iridescent silks. You can also find beautiful color complexity in wood furniture that has been hand-rubbed and hand-waxed, when a hint of the grain shows through. Most conveniently, complex colors tend to work rather gracefully with each other, as well as with more basic color elements. And their reaction to light is more compelling: each layer creates its own luminous palette.

Knowing how to use complex colors — boldly, sensuously, provocatively — is an important element in design fusion. I always begin with the proverbial blank canvas, choosing colors as though I were collaging a scrapbook of my fantasy room. One approach, which I used in my Hampton house, is to start with a base of neutrals — ivory, sand, parchment, driftwood, or slate. Think of using this palette for most of your bigger pieces of furniture and/or for your windows, walls, and flooring. And for a seamless effect, you can use the same color wash for both walls and windows.

Then, essentially, have fun. You can have one piece with a statement-making pattern or color — such as an oversized Thai coffee table with a hand-rubbed turquoise apron or a collection of boldly colored contemporary prints. But don't overlook smaller pieces — it's a myth that small pieces can't use bold patterns or colors. Bright African kente cloth looks fabulous on small wicker slipper chairs, and hand-blocked Indian print pillows can provide an interesting visual when strewn across a natural linen sofa.

You should also think about creating unusual color juxtapositions. As the color-field paintings of Barnett Newman, Marc Rothko, and Helen Frankenthaler brilliantly show, the true character of a color is revealed when intermixed with other, sometimes quite clashing shades. There really are no rules for color combos: blue and brown do work together; pink and red do work together. A dissonant color in a room is like a dissonant chord in a symphony: the result can be a charming, unexpected harmony.

The other approach is to make one color both your base and your statement, and then layer within the same color category. Again, layering colors works best when you use different textures. For instance, by combining a linen velvet, a rustic raffia, and a luminous silk — all from the same color family — you allow the color to deepen, creating far more visual complexity. I often dress like this by combining, for example, an olive skirt, a wasabi T-shirt, a khaki canvas jacket, sage suede shoes, and a breen (brown/green) leather bag — all different but related greens with an interesting variation in texture and finish.

Here are some examples of tonal colors that I find compelling:

- raisin, eggplant, mulberry, Bordeaux, oxblood
- eggshell, biscuit, chalk, putty, alabaster, twine, burlap
- sage, celadon, aloe, pistachio, artichoke, eucalyptus
- breen, khaki, tobacco, caper, lichen, seaweed
- mustard, bronze, curry, corn husk, vermeil, raw umber
- greige (gray/beige), wet cement, mink, slate, mushroom
- azure, cerulean, aquamarine, wisteria, seafoam
- cantaloupe, peach, tangerine, tea stain, apricot
- paprika, henna, burnt sienna, carnelian, persimmon, nutmeg

Finally, I don't believe there should be any outdoor/indoor distinctions regarding color and patterns. It is the geographical location and quality of light that will inspire your choices — what works on the east end of Long Island will be different from what works in the Arizona desert. Color, in fact, is a great way to bring the outdoors in, through the use of nature-inspired tones and textures. Color also allows you to create your own fantasy cocoon of warmth and safety, blocking out the outside environment entirely.

PRECEDING PAGES: A smorgasbord of vibrant colors is perfect for upholstery, contrast welts, hems, and alternate seam details on pillows; bohemian chic — personal statements can easily be made through the use of color.

ABOVE, FROM LEFT: The contrasting color peeking through on this chair leg displays the ultimate in design tension — the element of surprise; this fabric offers deep, saturated colors in a Baroque-meets-Byzantine design; silk damask, in a multitude of tone-on-tone jewellike colors; color can also be used to set a sultry yet regal mood.

Not coincidentally, colors that most closely resemble those found in nature tend to create the strongest emotional impact.

RIGHT: My office, redecorated for a Valentine's Day luncheon. The side chairs are upholstered in Donghia's interpretation of a traditional *ikat* weave, a process of warp printing that can be found in a variety of cultures. The table runner on the console is a patchwork of different strips of Sashiko, a jacquard inspired by the early-eighteenth-century Japanese custom of recycling pieces of old fabric through the use of fine running stitches. A striped kilim rug in matching colors anchors this vignette. Such a diversity of textures and patterns works best when they're linked through a tonal color scheme.

FOLLOWING PAGES: I always try to accessorize within related color families. At left, my collection of coral, which has inspired many of our deep earth tones. At right, some of my exotic bangles, which are often called into service as table jewelry.

ABOVE: The color palette of this handblown glass collection recalls seventeenth- and eighteenth-century Venetian glass. The flecks of gold leaf dispersed throughout add a layer of sparkle.
RIGHT: Color binds vintage remnants of paisley with our Sashiko fabric, recycling old with new.

ABOVE, FROM LEFT: Color inspirations, nestling here in a leather bowl; our multicolored Souk Stripe, which was inspired by the vibrant awning stripes of the bustling *souks*, or markets, of Egypt and Morocco; choked tassels in a multitude of colors; different patterns can work together if the colors are compatible.
PAGE 145: Amber and ochre tones tie together block-printed pillows, beeswax candles, Middle Eastern pottery, and two traditional Moroccan tables — all interestingly combined with our Mado table.

Knowing how to use complex colors — boldly, sensuously, provocatively — is an important element in design fusion.

PRECEDING PAGES: My country living room is able to embrace a variety of diverse textures and patterns with a tonal palette of ecru, terra-cotta, and tangerine. Contemporary Christo prints mix with a sandblasted amber lamp and Pavone drapery.

RIGHT: The color in my living room comes from the accessories. A custom chaise in natural linen displays a Swedish wedding blanket, an Indonesian *ikat* throw, and a hand-embroidered Afghani pillow, while a Cubana chair wears African kente cloth. More colorful accents come from the Turkish kilim and the hand-carved Thai coffee table, which has a turquoise apron and displays an Aboriginal *pitti* vessel carved from tree bark.

FOLLOWING PAGES: In the master bathroom, a mélange of spice tones are set off by two brushed silver vessels from Morocco. The chaise is covered in our whimsical Pavone, which features a rustic "folk art" peacock, and the old bamboo chair is covered with a hand-embroidered vest, found in a local antique shop.

ABOVE: Our Espadrille stripe with a vessel that sits on three glass bun feet. **RIGHT:** Chairs in various shades of Espadrille and a French country marble table combine nicely with a Guatemalan sideboard accessorized with an Alexander Calder print, a charm-covered box from the Sudan, a Burmese lacquer container, and an African Dogon headdress.

PRECEDING PAGES: In my bedroom, color, texture, and pattern become inseparable: my collection of rare Indonesian batik textiles mix with woven baskets and jewelry. My den features a sofa upholstered in a jacquard inspired by the traditional Japanese tie-dye technique called *shibori*. This is the only room in the house that we didn't whitewash; the natural pine — knots and all — works better with the more muted palette. **ABOVE:** In another guest room, I tacked a *thoran*, an authentic Indian door-hanging, across a bed headboard. **RIGHT:** An array of different textures joined by a neutral palette — a coin-encrusted Moroccan leather bag, a wicker chair with our Snappy fabric, Mado tables, Sachin pillows, and Guatemalan quilts.

CHAPTER EIGHT

Light

is to a home as optimism is to a person: everything else — great space, high-quality furnishings, brilliant artwork — feels somewhat uninspired without it.

It was the early seventies when I first discovered the eastern tip of Long Island. By then I had done quite

a bit of traveling, and was certainly no stranger to the inordinate beauty of cities like Istanbul and islands like Bali. Still, the endless mass of white, pristine beaches seduced me immediately. Whimsical seaside villages, vast flatlands of corn and potato fields, great forests of black pines — I fully understood why so many artists and writers have long been magnetically drawn to the area.

But of all the mystical aspects, it was the quality of the light, from sunrise to sunset, that first drew me under its spell. From the early morning rays filtering through the pine trees to the glowing halo permeating the misty dusk, the light on eastern Long Island is both transportive and illuminating, heightening all sensual awareness.

The night light of New York City offers a different sort of stimulation. With the bridges lit like pearl necklaces and the grids of windows in every tall building looking like checkerboard light boxes — New York City at night is a constant source of positive energy for me, of hope for another good day ahead.

Through the years I have come to believe that light is to a home as optimism is to a person: everything else — great space, high-quality furnishings, brilliant artwork — feels somewhat uninspired without it.

To make the most out of whatever natural light you have, I always suggest layering your windows, first with a sheer cotton, linen, or even cashmere scrim that will filter light in a very sensual way, and then with a heavier and more opaque fabric, such as silk, cotton, or wool. In my Tribeca living room, a fine cotton scrim in misty taupe diffuses the midday sun, while flannel-lined silk-and-linen draperies flank the window's sides as a soft architectural frame.

When deciding the yardage needed for draperies,

always overestimate for a more dramatic and rich result, and allow the fabric panels to graze the floor. To keep the focus on the soft vertical folds of drapery, I like to keep the hardware simple and tailored, using either oversized metal grommets with a metal rod threading through them or the classic seven-inch pinch pleat with a wood rod and round wooden rings.

Try to use as little strong overhead lighting as possible — not only does it absorb natural light, but it's also not very flattering. Better to have multiple sources of light at different heights — table lamps, floor lamps, sconces, and chandeliers — and on dimmers. There is such a great selection of bulbs today, you can create the type of light that works best for the diverse living requirements of each room: from tiny pin-spots to soft recessed uplighting.

Dark colors, matte surfaces, and pile weaves like chenille and velvet absorb the light, be it natural or synthetic, while light colors, shiny surfaces, and satin weaves reflect the light. For visual and tactile variety, try to have a balance of both.

Accessories should be thought of as light-enhancing jewelry for the room. Mirrors, for example, can't help but maximize light and space, essentially creating "another room" within your room.

While glass in general is intrinsically light-enhancing, the filmy fragility of handblown glass offers a warmer, more flattering reflection. I discovered the magic of light reflecting and filtering through handmade Venetian glass during my many design development trips to the small island of Murano, the center of production for Venice's treasured glassware since the thirteenth century. In the early years, Murano glass became such a lucrative commodity that the secrets of its production were protected by the Venetian government. I myself became an addict, so much so that most of my light sources are now from Murano in the form of table and floor lamps, chandeliers, and wall sconces.

The warmest, most flattering glow of all, of course, can come only from candlelight. I was first awakened to its seductive power on Christmas Eve some decades ago. Sitting in the choir loft above all the flickering points of light, I was in complete awe! To this day, I use candles of all sizes to create the most romantic settings.

And there is nothing more enchanting than a combination of candlelight and mirrors: you will truly feel transported to a different century. In fact, in eighteenth-century France, the perimeters of a room — door frames, wainscoting, windows, and so on — were outlined in gold leaf so as to be able to catch the candle's reflection in the most optimal way. Imagine the candlelit rooms of that era, flickering in and out of focus, looking like line drawings in golden ink.

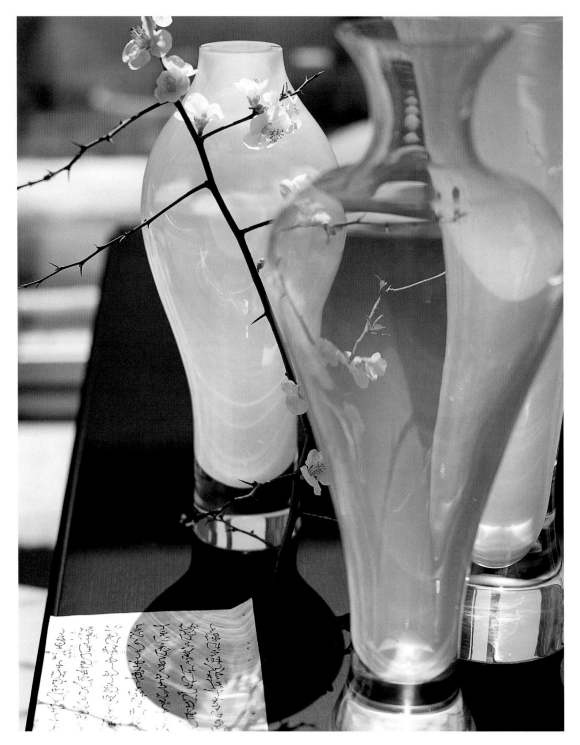

PAGE 159: Like the pearl, the making of glass begins with a grain of sand. The process can be traced back to 50 BC: ancient Phoenicians discovered that when they subjected sand to extreme heat, it miraculously produced a new substance with the seemingly incongruous qualities of durability and fragility. **ABOVE:** Light brings clarity and a sense of timeless space to a room. Handblown glass distinctively reflects and refracts light, creating a lyrical, near-magical aura. **RIGHT:** Fabric and finish can reflect light as well. On these chairs, the luminescent quality of the fabric and the platinum leaf finish enhance the beauty of this room's effusive natural light.

RIGHT: Integrating mirrors not only adds depth to any room, it also augments the sources of light. Mirrors don't have to be hung: leaning them on a table or floor creates an added dimension, not to mention visual interest.

FOLLOWING PAGES: The translucency of handblown glass brilliantly diffuses light, producing an exquisitely ethereal effect; a white sheer linen slipcover on our Ghost chair can create the same airy, otherworldly delicacy.

ABOVE: Our Egg Vessel brilliantly reflects the light from a nearby window. The centuries-old craft of Venetian glassblowing produces singular works of collectible art — no two pieces are exactly alike. **RIGHT:** The flecks of gold leaf dispersed throughout the glass bowl further enhance its reflective qualities. Here it holds a set of floating tealights, creating the most dramatic and flattering light of all. **FOLLOWING PAGES:** Neutral or monochromatic interiors diffuse and soften the light. The column is covered in our Hammered Silver wallcovering, adding another dimension of shimmery reflection. Donghia's Stellare chandelier presents classical, clean lines with a contemporary twist.

PAGES 172–173: Double layers of glass give these lamps an enchanted air; a set of Athena lamps offers the most subtle hint of color. Layering provides the best tool for manipulating light. **PRECEDING PAGES:** Our Laser Scrim is coated on the reverse side with stainless steel powder, producing a metallic, shimmery effect. I love combining this high-tech fabric with a wide border of heavy rustic linen. An amber lamp subtly illuminates an unpretentious wooden tray. **ABOVE AND RIGHT:** Mirrors open up space, creating a room within a room. It takes one artisan one week to complete each of our Venetian glass mirrors, whose slightly patinated surface creates a warmer (and more flattering) cast.

ABOVE AND RIGHT: Our Cat's Cradle casement, inspired by a vintage crocheted dress, hangs over the outside door in one of my country guest bathrooms, allowing both light and privacy. The yarn is embroidered onto a paperlike, non-woven ground, then washed in a special bath, leaving only the beautiful spider-web-like embroidery behind.

There is nothing more enchanting than a combination of candlelight and mirrors: you will truly feel transported to a different century.

ABOVE, FROM LEFT: Don't forget the reflective quality of metals. Under the glass surface of my coffee table lies an eighteenth-century Indian textile, with handcrafted metal *zari* embroidery; perfect for windows and walls, Donghia's Mirror Mirror fabric, which combines handwoven Dupioni silk with the centuries-old embroidery techniques of Indian artisans, throws magical spots of light across the room as it is adorned with tiny circular mirrors; hand-twisted cords of precious metals offer an understated opulence to any piece — think of them as jewelry for your home.

CHAPTER NINE

Natural evolutions keep a home's spirit alive and its character enhanced.

All things are incomplete — in a constant, never-ending state of becoming or dissolving: the aim is progress, not perfection. That's one of the central tenets of Wabi Sabi, and I have found it particularly useful when dealing with life's inevitable frustrations and disappointments. Obstacles can better be seen as challenges, meant to enlighten and embolden, and our minor "imperfections" can be both exploited and cherished: they are what make us unique and beautiful.

If our home is truly going to be an extension of ourselves, then it too must progress, evolving as we evolve. A room frozen in time, with no sign of human life or activity, can only look and feel stagnant, dispirited, oppressive.

If you see your home as a continual work in progress, you will naturally begin to think critically and creatively about each room — adding pieces that you can't live without and editing out what doesn't work or no longer suits you.

• Keep collecting what you love, and move your collections around to give things a new prominence. Give your latest passion room to breathe by putting other items in storage.

• Treat your storage containers as beautiful display pieces. I always use lacquer boxes, handmade baskets, silver trays, and wooden bowls to keep all my treasured possessions.

• Move artwork around, and don't assume it always has to be hanging on a wall. You can lean it on floors, window ledges, or single dining chairs. Or prop it in an out-of-season fireplace. Unusual locations will only enhance its presence.

• Seasonally dress and undress your home: bedding, slipcovers, carpets, throws, draperies, and door-hangings can easily be swapped for a completely different look.

• Think about "jewelry" for your home. I sometimes hang beads, tassels, ribbons, belts, and handbags on doorknobs, hooks, and drapery finials for a very personal, whimsical touch.

• Don't forget to "recycle" — move pieces between home and office or (if you're lucky) between homes. It's amazing how a new location can inspire a new attitude. I have moved my favorite silver Indian table, my Indonesian cabinet, my African inlaid wood table, and my vintage Donghia faux-ivory table from room to room in my three different New York apartments — and some eventually went to my country house!

Design evolution is all about further enhancing your home's character, exposing more of its soul. You can buy magnificent pieces from all over the world and fuse them in the most innovative, textured manner. But a home's poetry — its internal beauty — can only come from your enduring emotional engagement.

Enjoy the process, and it will forever captivate and inspire you.

Sherri Donghia joined Donghia Furniture/Textiles Ltd. in 1987, after a unique career in the international fashion world. She began at Bloomingdale's under Katherine Murphy and then moved on to Federated Department Stores before starting her own design and consulting firm.

She is currently the Executive Vice President/Creative Director of Donghia, Inc., where she oversees the focused design direction of the Donghia companies and continually provides a cohesive vision for the multiple categories of interior furnishings. Sherri has built a reputation as a renowned textile editor, winning numerous international industry awards: in 2001 she was the first American to be awarded the prestigious Master of Linen award by the European Union's Masters of Linen group; she became the US recipient of the first *Elle Decor* Design Award for Textiles; and she has received the Chicago Athenaeum's Good Design Award for four years (2001–2004) for outstanding product design.

Beyond her dedication to Donghia, Sherri guest lectures at design schools internationally, mentors students, chairs the interiors committee of the Color Association of the United States (CAUS), and is on the board of Aid-to-Artisans (ATA) as well as Fashion Group International (FGI).

acknowledgments

Books have always been part of my most treasured possessions; they serenely sit in nearly every room of my two homes, and they line the entire back wall of my office. The opportunity to create my own book — stemming from years of looking at and thinking about every aspect of design — has been thoroughly rewarding on so many levels. Most of all, it has given me the opportunity to display in one beautiful, sensual package the brilliance of the extraordinary people I work and live with. For helping to make this dream a reality, I would like to extend a special thanks to:

My mother and father, who have always given me confidence, support, and inspiration to reach for the stars.

Roger Eulau, my husband, partner, trusted soul mate, and gifted chef and photographer.

The late Mrs. Carmella Donghia, who I know would have appreciated this effort more than anyone, and who set many examples for all who knew her to follow.

Angelo, who started the Donghia design legacy by following his passion for living well and enjoying the best that life has to offer every day. We continually draw inspiration from his brilliant work and innovative ideas.

Vera Vandenbosch, my marketing director and tireless associate and friend, for working side by side with me on every aspect of this adventure.

The entire Donghia creative team: Lori Barra, Candice Eng, Jennifer Hutton, Allison Kettlewell, Jason Lowe, Julia Membrino, Jimmy Mitchell, Pamela Muccini, Randall Phelan, Kerri Quillin, Feliks Rabinovich, Aviva Shulem, and last but not least, Masaru Suzuki, a living example of the artistry of luxury and style.

The dedicated Donghia sales and support teams around the world, for their hard work and sincere passion, especially Brian Hackfeld, who travels the farthest!

Susan Slover and her team for decades of creative collaboration on unique Donghia visuals.

The Bulfinch Press team, especially Jill Cohen and Kristen Schilo for their timely vision and ideas.

Doug Turshen, our truly inspired art director and designer.

Karen Lehrman, intelligent writer and patient listener.

Richard Giglio, talented artist and good friend.

Nelsa Gidney and Jordan Ringel for the generous use of their handsome home.

All the photographers who have so generously shared their material for this book: Roger Davies, Pieter Estersohn, Roger E. Eulau, Scott Frances, Oberto Gili, Michael Grimm, Maura McEvoy, James Merrell, Bärbel Miebach, Michael Mundy, Laura Resen, David Sawyer, Joe Standart, Wouter Vandertol, Peter Vitale, William Waldron, and especially Edward Addeo, a talented and loyal Donghia collaborator for over a decade.

Our textile mills, who make our wildest design dreams a reality.

The Donghia furniture makers, especially Vito Ursini, every one of them a highly skilled artisan with a true love and appreciation for the craft of fine upholstery and woodworking.

The Venetian glass artisans in Murano, Italy, the ultimate master craftsmen who realize our designs one piece at a time.

And finally, a profound and heartfelt thank-you to the Rubelli family for continuing Donghia's design legacy for generations to come.

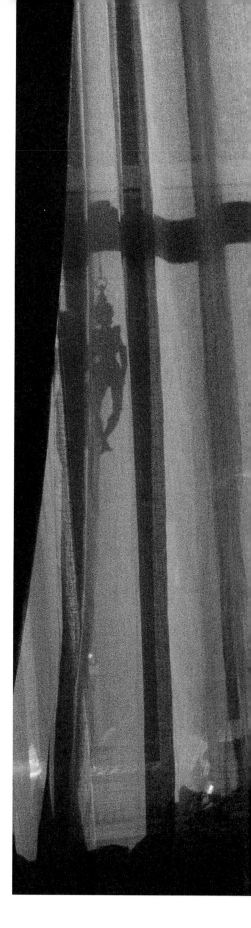

index

Bulfinch Press

Hachette Book Group USA
1271 Avenue of the Americas, New York, NY 10020
Visit our Web site at www.bulfinchpress.com

First Edition: October 2006

Library of Congress Cataloging-in-Publication Data

Donghia, Sherri.
    Donghia : the artistry of luxury and style / Sherri
        Donghia. — 1st ed.
        p. cm.
    Includes index.
    ISBN-10: 0-8212-5791-9 (hardcover)
    ISBN-13: 978-0-8212-5791-3 (hardcover)
    1. Donghia Furniture/Textiles Ltd. 2. Donghia, Sherri.
3. Interior decoration — United States. I. Title.

NK2004.3.D66A4 2006
749.092 — dc22   2005033362

Designed by Doug Turshen with David Huang

PRINTED IN SINGAPORE